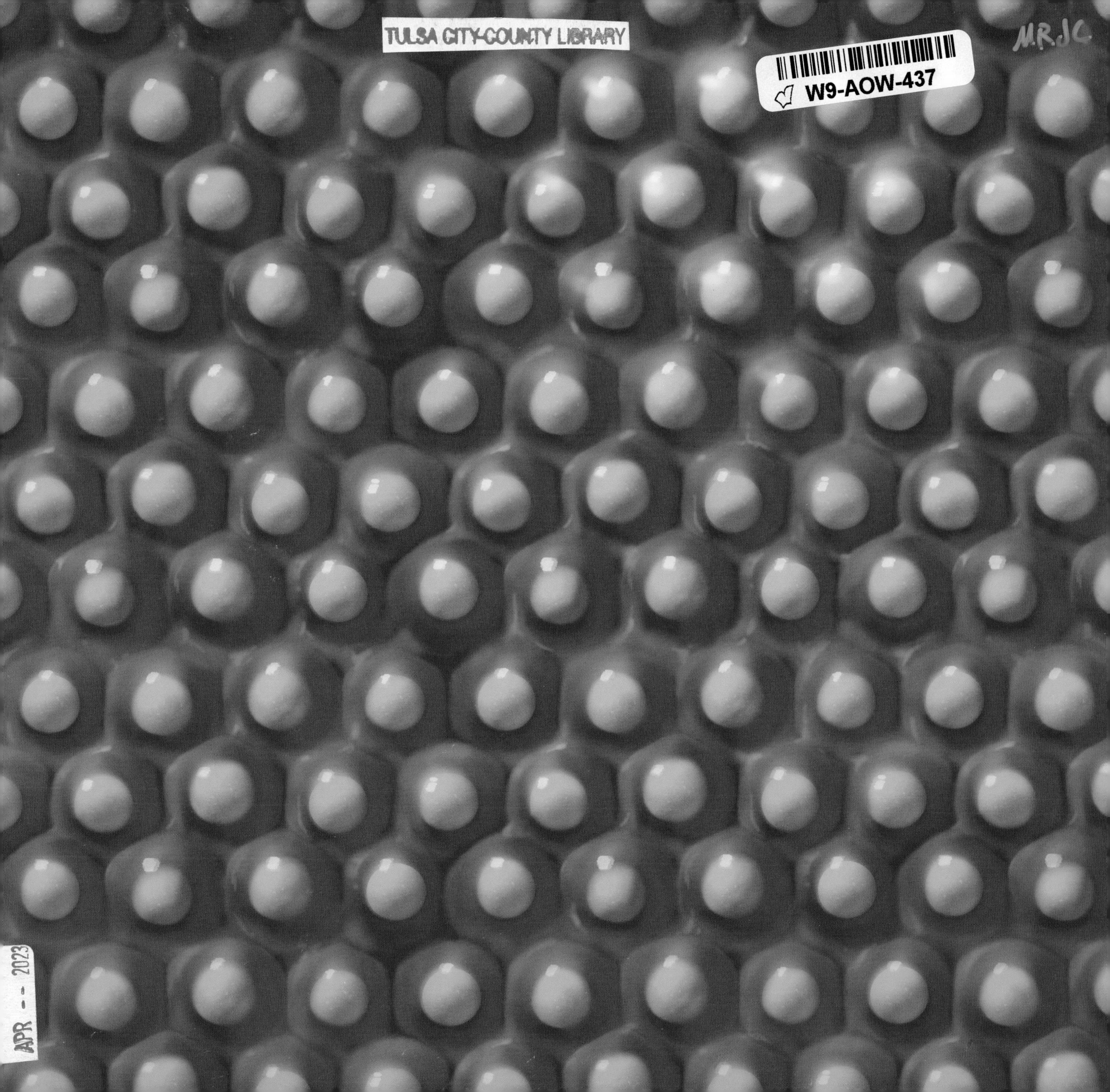

To my mother's garden, the place where I first
became enchanted by the small wonders of nature
TP

To Massi, who taught me to love Costa Rica,
and to my mom, who taught me to love science
MJ

ONE
TINY TREEFROG

A COUNTDOWN TO SURVIVAL

Tony Piedra & Mackenzie Joy

CANDLEWICK PRESS

Ten tiny tadpoles
grow in their eggs.

adult red-eyed treefrog
(*Agalychnis callidryas*)

Nine alert tadpoles
begin to wiggle free.

social wasp
(*Polybia rejecta*)

WIGGLE

WIGGLE

Eight wriggling tadpoles

P

LUNGE

plink

plink

wolf cichlid
(*Parachromis dovii*)

plink

. . . into a watery new home.

carmine skimmer
dragonfly nymph
(*Orthemis discolor*)

Seven wary tadpoles
learn to hide.

Six little tadpoles
peek above the pool.

carmine skimmer
(*Orthemis discolor*)

Five growing tadpoles start to

Four strong tadpoles
surface for a breath of air.

Three quick tadpoles

JUMP!

bare-throated tiger heron
(*Tigrisoma mexicanum*)

Two nimble tadpoles
prepare to leave the water.

young spectacled caiman
(*Caiman crocodilus*)

One resilient tadpole
sees something familiar...

Zero tiny tadpoles.

One tiny treefrog.

What does it take to become one tiny **red-eyed treefrog?**

(Agalychnis callidryas)

It takes a whole lot of eggs!

Red-eyed treefrogs do not care for their young, so laying many eggs is a survival strategy. The more eggs a mother frog lays, the greater the chances that one will beat the odds to grow into a treefrog.

This story starts with ten eggs, but red-eyed treefrogs usually lay clutches of closer to forty eggs on leaves that overhang ponds or temporary pools of water. When it is time to hatch, the new tadpoles wiggle free from their eggs and drop into the water below. For about nine weeks, they live a completely aquatic life and undergo dramatic physical changes, transforming from tadpoles into tiny froglets in a process called metamorphosis. As adults, red-eyed treefrogs never return to the water. Instead, they live high up in the trees and are active only at night.

Our story takes place in the lowland wet forests of Costa Rica, and all the animals and plants in this book are found in or near the ponds, lakes, and rivers of this small, biodiverse, and beautiful country. Costa Rica makes up just 0.03 percent of the world's land-mass, but it is home to more than 5 percent of the world's species: more than 12,000 plants, 800 birds, 400 reptiles and amphibians, 200 mammals, and 175 freshwater fish! Over a quarter of Costa Rica's lands are protected in the form of national parks, biological reserves, and wildlife refuges—some of the most of any country in the world. Sadly, many species are still endangered.

Can you spot all the Costa Rican species that appeared in the book?

1. rhinoceros katydid
(*Copiphora rhinoceros*)

2. cauque river prawn
(*Macrobrachium americanum*)

3. social wasp
(*Polybia rejecta*)

4. carmine skimmer
(*Orthemis discolor*)

5. wolf cichlid
(*Parachromis dovii*)

6. bare-throated tiger heron
(*Tigrisoma mexicanum*)

7. lined tree snail
(*Drymaeus tripictus*)

8. apricot sulphur butterfly
(*Phoebis argante*)

9. spectacled caiman
(*Caiman crocodilus*)

10. leafcutter ant
(*Atta cephalotes*)

11. three-striped firefly
(*Photuris trivittata*)

12. northern cat-eyed snake
(*Leptodeira septentrionalis*)

13. livebearer fish
(*Brachyrhaphis rhabdophora*)

Surviving to Become One Tiny Treefrog

 Ten • Red-eyed treefrogs are nocturnal amphibians that lay their eggs on leaves overhanging ponds and puddles. Scientists have observed that red-eyed treefrogs typically lay clutches of forty to as many as one hundred eggs at a time.

 Nine • Red-eyed treefrog embryos can sense the vibrations around them and are even able to tell the difference between harmless events, like rain or wind, and dangerous events, like the approach of hungry predators. Under normal conditions, embryos hatch in about a week, but they can hatch early if they sense a threat. Snakes and wasps account for over half of red-eyed treefrog embryo predation.

 Eight • Embryos normally hatch in six to eight days—frequently during a downpour—falling like drops of rain into the water below. This camouflaging behavior is believed to help hide them from potential predators and so increase their chances of survival. A scientific study in Costa Rica found that only 63 percent of embryos survive to become tadpoles.

 Seven • Dragonfly nymphs are tiny aquatic predators of red-eyed treefrog tadpoles. Just like frogs, dragonflies go through dramatic physical changes between hatching and adulthood in a process called metamorphosis. This nymph is the larval stage of a carmine skimmer dragonfly.

 Six • The treefrog is often described as tiny, but that's only true when compared to a larger species, like us (*Homo sapiens*). In fact, the female adult red-eyed treefrog is typically 2–2¾ inches/51–71 millimeters long. Adult males are smaller, at 1–2¼ inches/30–59 millimeters. At almost 2 inches/48 millimeters, red-eyed treefrog tadpoles are considered large, longer than some adult males.

 Five • When they are about thirty days old, red-eyed treefrog tadpoles start to sprout rear legs as they go through metamorphosis. Some tadpoles develop more slowly than others, making them more susceptible to predation. Two of the most successful predators of red-eyed treefrog tadpoles are the livebearer fish and the cauque river prawn.

 Four • For the first two weeks of their lives, tadpoles breathe underwater like fish, using their gills to capture oxygen. But as they undergo metamorphosis, their gills degenerate and lungs grow, forming muscles and cartilage to facilitate the pumping of air. At this stage in their development, the tadpoles are considered froglets and they must surface to breathe.

 Three • As froglets mature, they spend less time in the water and face a new set of terrestrial predators, including the bare-throated tiger heron. Studies of red-eyed treefrogs in captivity show that full metamorphosis takes sixty to eighty days. Less is known about what happens in the wild because, as a nocturnal, tree-dwelling species, red-eyed treefrogs are difficult to observe. Science is constantly learning and correcting itself as new discoveries are made. Who knows what exciting discoveries will be made in the future!

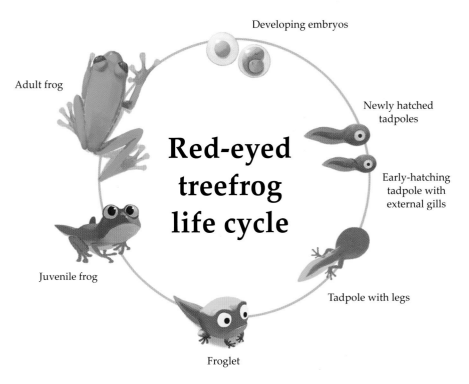

Red-eyed treefrog life cycle

Developing embryos

Newly hatched tadpoles

Early-hatching tadpole with external gills

Tadpole with legs

Froglet

Juvenile frog

Adult frog

Two • While the book depicts hungry predators, like the baby spectacled caiman, treefrog tadpoles are all about eating. Metamorphosis takes so much energy that they must eat constantly to sustain their growth. As tadpoles, they are mostly herbivorous, grazing on green algae and decaying, suspended vegetation. As adults, they become carnivorous, feeding on insects like crickets, flies, grasshoppers, and moths. They have even been known to eat smaller frogs.

One • You might be wondering why the young red-eyed treefrogs in this book do not have red eyes until the last page. The red-eyed treefrog's eyes do not become red and its body does not develop its famous color pattern until the frog matures. The red coloration first appears at the edge of the eye, about two weeks post-metamorphosis, and over several days spreads inward to make the whole eye red.

Zero • Red-eyed treefrogs can be found in the lowland wet forests of Central America, from the Yucatán to northern Colombia. The red-eyed treefrogs shown in this book live in Costa Rica. Many illustrated books and documentary films about nature present viewers a world without signs of human civilization. Even if you travel deep into the Costa Rican rain forest, however, evidence of human presence can be seen, from subtle footpaths to hanging bridges to distant cell towers to lights from nearby towns. We have included signs of human civilization in our art as a reminder that, while much wilderness and wildlife remains, humans are never far away.

Selected Bibliography

Caldwell, Michael S., J. Gregory McDaniel, and Karen Warkentin. "Is It Safe? Red-Eyed Treefrog Embryos Assessing Predation Risk Use Two Features of Rain Vibrations to Avoid False Alarms." *Animal Behaviour*, vol. 79, no. 2 (2010): 255–260. https://doi.org/10.1016/j.anbehav.2009.11.005.

Warkentin, Karen M. "Effects of Hatching Age on Development and Hatchling Morphology in the Red-Eyed Tree Frog, *Agalychnis Callidryas*." *Biological Journal of the Linnean Society*, vol. 68, no. 3 (1999): 443–470. https://doi.rg/10.1111/j.1095-8312.1999.tb01180.x.

Warkentin, Karen M. "Wasp Predation and Wasp-Induced Hatching of Red-Eyed Treefrog Eggs." *Animal Behaviour*, vol. 60, no. 4 (2000): 503–510. https://doi.org/10.1006/anbe.2000.1508.

Suggested Further Reading and Viewing

For a comprehensive guide to the amphibians and reptiles of Costa Rica: Savage, Jay Mathers. *The Amphibians and Reptiles of Costa Rica: A Herpetofauna between Two Continents, between Two Seas.* Chicago: University of Chicago Press, 2002.

For a glimpse at the amphibians, reptiles, and insects that live in the tropics: Naskrecki, Piotr. *The Smaller Majority: The Hidden World of the Animals That Dominate the Tropics.* Cambridge, MA: Belknap Press of Harvard University Press, 2005.

Check out one of our favorite books, a guide to all the plants and animals that call Earth home: Hennessy, Kathryn, and Smithsonian Institution, eds. *Natural History: The Ultimate Visual Guide to Everything on Earth.* New York: DK, 2010.

Watch the incredible development of an alpine newt embryo from a single cell into a complex living organism in "Becoming" by Jan van IJken, copyright 2017. https://vimeo.com/316043706.